Capturing ess   ly winsome style of s   e- lationships as insi   ng relationship with ı   ns and homey personal experiences to weave three central teachings of Lutheranism into a beautiful theological tapestry. This is no dreary doctrinaire discourse, but a warm armchair conversation with a friend who delightfully engages you with his scriptural-based narratives of grace and faith. It was a joy to read each chapter as they related to my own life, and it's certainly worth sharing with others.

Rev. Dr. Timothy Maschke,
emeritus professor of theology,
Concordia University Wisconsin

Dr. Paavola has taken the great heavenly ideas of the Lutheran Reformation (Scripture alone, grace alone, and faith alone) and brought them down to earth in this wonderfully profound and accessible book. With a mix of story, analogy, and scriptural truth, these pages serve up a delightful appetizer to the meal that is Lutheran theology. For anyone curious about what it means to be Lutheran, this book will prove to be a valuable introduction. For the seasoned Lutheran, it will provide a delightful reminder of the joy we have in our relationship with Jesus Christ.

Rev. Bob Hiller,
senior pastor of Community Lutheran Church,
content editor for www.craftofpreaching.org.

Grace, Faith, Scripture by Daniel Paavola is a "Portrait of a Lutheran" in two ways. In his own winsome, conversational, and faithful way, he shows how grace alone, faith alone, and Scripture alone were and are essential for his own spiritual life and relationships. He also shows through personal story and Scripture how these foundational slogans of the Lutheran Reformation actively paint the portrait of any faithful, Bible-based, confessional Lutheran in his or her life of faith under the cross of Christ in Word and Sacrament. For some, *Grace, Faith, Scripture* will be an introduction to the Lutheran confession of the Christian faith. For others, it will serve as encouragement to remain faithful to our confession, dig deeper in God's Word, and walk together with Christ alongside Paul, Luther, Walther, and the author in the pure Gospel of Jesus Christ.

Rev. Paul Cain,
editor, Lutheran book reviewer,
pastor at Immanuel Lutheran Church

GRACE

PORTRAIT

FAITH

OF A LUTHERAN

SCRIPTURE

DANIEL E. PAAVOLA

CONCORDIA PUBLISHING HOUSE · SAINT LOUIS

Concordia
Publishing House

Published by Concordia Publishing House

3558 S. Jefferson Ave., St. Louis, MO 63118-3968

1-800-325-3040 ● www.cph.org

Cover photo by Rev. Paul T. McCain

Manufactured in the United States of America

Library of Congress Cataloging-in-Publication Data
Names: Paavola, Daniel E., author.
Title: Grace, faith, scripture : portrait of a Lutheran / Daniel Paavola.
Description: Saint Louis : Concordia Publishing House, 2019.
Identifiers: LCCN 2018059094 (print) | LCCN 2019018722 (ebook) | ISBN 9780758662439 () | ISBN 9780758662422
Subjects: LCSH: Spirituality--Lutheran Church. | Lutheran Church--Doctrines.
Classification: LCC BX8065.3 (ebook) | LCC BX8065.3 .P33 2019 (print) | DDC 230/.41--dc23
LC record available at https://lccn.loc.gov/2018059094

1 2 3 4 5 6 7 8 9 10   28 27 26 25 24 23 22 21 20 19

CONTENTS

ACKNOWLEDGMENTS

Lutherans are both unique and ordinary. Certainly, we have a distinctive heritage with Martin Luther and all those who came after him who upheld the faith as expressed in the Lutheran Confessions. But Lutherans are centered on three aspects of Christianity that are essential to the faith of all Christians. We are people of the Bible, basing our faith on God's Word alone. In that Word, we find that grace alone is the central message of God in His relationship with us. To accept that gift, we need faith alone. Those three—Scripture, grace, and faith—are Lutheran hallmarks; however, they are also God's gifts to all Christians.

This book uses the three gifts of Scripture, grace, and faith as an introduction to the Lutheran faith. If you are a Lutheran already, I hope this strengthens your understanding of the faith and gives you ways to express it to others. If you are not yet a Lutheran, here is your invitation to understand us better and to share these same gifts from God with us.

Thank you to the many at Concordia Publishing House for their creative work on this project. Special thanks go to Laura Lane and Scot Kinnaman, whose careful editing and creative ideas make every page better. Thank you to my colleagues and friends at Concordia University Wisconsin for their support. Finally, thanks go to my family: to my wife, Holly, and to our three children, Christy, Steve, and Nicole, for being the center of these stories about relationships.

They are a model of relationships, centered on grace, lived by faith.

Blessings to you as you read His Word, with its message of grace received by faith.

CHAPTER 1

THESE THREE KEEP US TOGETHER

People know only so much about you. Your neighbors, the people at work, even your friends—they all know only a part of you. However, what they know paints their picture of you. My neighbors know that I love motorcycles and ride almost every day. They know I teach at Concordia University, but they might not know I teach theology. They know I go running most days, and they remember that I used to run a lot faster. That's about it. It's not the whole picture, but it starts the sketch.

What do people know about you? It could be that you faithfully leave for work every morning at 5:00 a.m. Maybe they know that beautiful red 1970 Chevy Nova that you drive on sunny days. Or perhaps they remember your kindness of mowing the lawn and shoveling the snow for the widow next door. Those few things are the sketch of you, a version of you that others would be glad to get to know better.

That's the purpose of this book. We'll outline a few things about Lutherans that start the picture of who we are. Those few things aren't the whole story of Lutherans, but I hope that they will make you want to fill in more of the picture, add colors and texture, give some depth and perspective. But to start, let's get three main points down.

IT'S THE STORY OF GOD'S RELATIONSHIP WITH US

A book about Lutherans is a book about a relationship: God's relationship with us and our unique understanding of that relationship. A story simply about Lutherans might be interesting, but we would be nothing more than another group of people with a distinctive spiritual understanding and history. That sentence alone sounds dull. The good news is that Lutherans tell their story through the relationship God has established with us. It's God's actions for us that make this relationship. God's actions of grace and mercy, His words, and His gifts are not the exclusive property of Lutherans, of course, but Lutherans love to tell the story of those gifts. Through those actions of God, all people are invited into this relationship with Him. This story is not only the Lutheran story, but it is also the story of God's actions that make His relationship with the world. These few points sketch the portrait of Lutherans, but they could be a sketch of you also.

Since we're speaking of a relationship, we'll be going over a story of growing relationships. Relationships grow slowly from first words through first dates to wondering if this is all going to go somewhere. Then come the big steps of marriage and that first home together. However, through all those changes, some constants hold two people together. There are first words that are never forgotten, acts of kindness that show someone's heart, and the trust that all we've begun won't simply end. Those points also tell the story of God's relationship with us and our unique understanding of it.

FIRST WORDS FIRST

Relationships begin with someone saying the first word. Before the words, there might be a smile that gives you hope. However, the relationship really won't start until someone says, "Hello." Maybe you remember the words that began a relationship that's still going today. You might still say those words to each other as a secret code between the two of you.

Lutherans focus on the first words in our relationship with God. God speaks those words to begin this relationship, and those are the words we remember and repeat. The good news is that they aren't a secret code; rather, they are the same open words that can be read by everyone. Our relationship with God stands on His Word alone. Lutherans speak of this dependence on God's Word with the Latin phrase *sola Scriptura*, meaning "Scripture alone." By this, Lutherans mean that our faith and our doctrine are founded solely on the words of the Bible. We'll speak much more on the key messages we find in the Bible, but for now, it's enough to celebrate this relationship that is begun and centered on His words to us.

"I'VE GOT ONE THING TO SAY TO YOU"

How does that sentence strike you? Of course, it depends on how someone says it, but imagine someone texting you that message. If you text me, "I've got one thing to say to you," I'm nervous. What? Why? What did I do? If someone has one thing to say to me, I'm sure it's going to be bad. And if that one thing is going to be the center of our relationship, then I'm not sure I want any part of it.

However, the wonderful news is that at its heart, the one thing God has to say is *grace*. Since we grow in relationship with God by what He says to us, then the greatest gift

Grace, Faith, Scripture

is that His message is one of mercy. God's grace is our second main point, called *sola gratia*, or "grace alone." By this phrase "grace alone," Lutherans mean that the central message of God is one of forgiveness. If forgiveness is received, that means forgiveness is needed. Our need to be forgiven of serious wrongs certainly is part of God's message. But God points out our sin in His Word not as an end in itself. The one thing God has to say is not, "You're condemned!" The central message of God is that we are saved by the forgiveness of our sins. John 3:17 is an example of His single intention: "For God did not send His Son into the world to condemn the world, but in order that the world might be saved through Him."

This second point in our relationship, grace alone, is the reason we can dare to hear the first point, the Word of God. In a wonderful relationship of committed love, you know you're going to solve your problems, settle the argument, and go to sleep in peace. You might even risk saying something serious: "We should talk about . . ." When you know that you're going to finish with "I love you; it will all work out," then you dare to talk.

Grace alone makes us bold to hear God's Word. We're like the thief on the cross, hanging beside Jesus on Good Friday. He knew that Jesus was the heavenly King and that He ruled in mercy. He dared to say in faith, "Jesus, remember me when You come into Your kingdom" (Luke 23:42). Jesus assured him, "Truly, I say to you, today you will be with Me in paradise" (Luke 23:43). When our words with God are few, they can center on His mercy and grace.

> When our words with God
> are few, they can center on
> His mercy and grace.

BUT ARE YOU SURE?

When I was sixteen, I backed our car out of the garage into our wide-open farmyard. I didn't look back. Why should I? There was never anything in the middle of the yard. Nothing, except the brand-new blue Dodge Dart belonging to my father's best friend, Otto. He had just brought it over to show my dad. I backed right into the Dart's front fender, never knowing it was there until that sickening feeling of my car stopping with metal crunching. I couldn't believe what I had done. But there was no denying it and nothing to do but walk into the house and tell Dad and Otto what had happened. In five minutes, my Dad went through three stages: "I can't believe you did this"; "You better start watching where you back up"; and "All right, let's get this fixed." After a trip to the body shop, Dad never said a word about it again.

You've had to walk into that kitchen too, I'm sure. It's hard to admit what we've done. Our inclination is to run. Deny, lie, or cry, but don't admit what you just did. If you dare to walk into the kitchen, you'd better be sure it will turn out all right. That takes faith. That is our third key point, *sola fide*, by faith alone. Faith is the gift God gives us in the reading of His Word and learning of His grace. Hearing His Word both gives faith and takes faith. Romans 10:17 tells us the first point: "So faith comes from hearing, and hearing through the word of Christ." By hearing the promises of God's grace, we believe those promises. If someone were to ask, "How do you know this?" our answer is, "Because I read what God said." We believe the promises of His mercy because they are His promises; they bring the power to believe them. It's more than wishful thinking, because His promises of complete forgiveness and eternal life are beyond our imagination. Because the life, death, and resurrection of Jesus are so extraordinary, they bring faith with them.

These three points of the Word alone, grace alone, and faith alone are enough to start describing the relationship God has with us. As we said at the start, no one knows everything about us. Your 5:00 a.m. departure for work, your overly friendly black Lab, and the fact that you have the most organized garage in town might be all they know. But it's a start. So it is with us Lutherans; you can tell a lot about us through these three things. We are people centered on God's Word, hearing His grace above all, and trusting in that grace by faith alone.

THE PERFECT MEAL

Relationships often revolve around food. Food can create the atmosphere in which a relationship grows. We'll use this food-relationship connection throughout the book. We're following the three keys, the three *solas*, of Lutheran faith. These essentials can remind us of the three essentials to a good meal at a restaurant. First, you need a menu that's understandable with food you want to eat. God's Word is clear and understandable as it gives us exactly the spiritual food we need. It gives us the balanced meal of Law and Gospel. Second, after reading the menu, you need to know the cost. The menu might describe a great meal, but can you afford it? You can if someone has already paid the bill. That would be grace. By grace, God pays for our entire bill. His payment on the cross was long before we knew our debt, but God accounted His Son's death as equal to all that we owed. Third, it's important to enjoy the meal and the relationship that comes with it. That takes faith. It's a bold thing to believe that the bill has been paid and you can actually enjoy the food. By faith alone, we can spend the most precious gift, time with God, and know that it has all been purchased already. Enjoy the meal; read the menu of His Word, all paid for by grace, and take that gift by faith.

> Enjoy the meal; read the menu of His Word, all paid for by grace, and take that gift by faith.

1. What three things do people most likely know about you? What would you add to that list?

2. Lutherans start with the Word of God alone. What Bible stories or biblical people express the central message of the Bible for you?

3. Lutherans believe that the Bible is clear and can be read by everyone. If so, how can you grow in your understanding of God's Word?

4. Grace is the mercy of God toward us. Why is this mercy needed in order for us to read the Word of God?

5. God's central message is His mercy and His desire to save the world (John 3:17). If God wants this relationship and result, why do we need to read about it?

6. This chapter told the story of the time I backed up into Otto's car. It took faith to walk into the kitchen and tell my dad what happened. When have you needed similar faith?

7. Faith comes by hearing God's promises. How can hearing the promises of God's mercy create faith?

RESOURCES

For further study and understanding, please consult the following resources.

Luther's Small Catechism with Explanation (St. Louis: Concordia Publishing House, 2017). For an overview of the faith, note especially Luther's brief explanations, pages 13–29.

For a more extensive treatment by Martin Luther, see the Large Catechism as found in *Concordia: The Lutheran Confessions*, second edition (St. Louis: Concordia Publishing House, 2006).

Lutheran Service Book, hymn 954: "We All Believe in One True God."

PART I

SCRIPTURE ALONE:

OUR RELATIONSHIP BEGINS WITH A WORD

CHAPTER 2

God Says
the First Word

My wife, Holly, says I don't remember the first words we said to each other. She's right; I don't. I don't remember exactly what I said, and no, I don't remember what she was wearing either, but I know she looked great. She remembers what I was wearing, but that's not fair. All through college I wore the same corduroy jean jacket with a grey hooded sweatshirt underneath. She shouldn't get credit for remembering that. But I do remember where we first spoke, and that should count for something. We were students at Minnesota State University at Moorhead, Minnesota. I was walking past the doors to the dining hall, and there she was, waiting for a friend. With no cell phones with which to distract ourselves in 1978, she was looking around, and I walked up and started talking.

What did I say? I'm sure it wasn't even as clever as, "Do you eat here often?" We probably only talked a minute. I don't know if we even exchanged names. We just stopped talking, and I walked away. But it certainly wasn't the last talk we've had.

Maybe you remember the first words that started your friendship. You have the exact time and place down, and you both even agree on how it started. If you can remember how she was wearing her hair that day, you're really something. However, whether you remember what you wore, what you said, and how you laughed, somehow it started with a word. You can look across the room at each other all you want, but nothing really happens until someone says, "Hello."

So it is with God's relationship with us. Our relationship depends on His first word. We can imagine God, but we'll have no relationship with Him until He begins the conversation. The key is that He first spoke to us, and by doing that He let us know His relationship with us. That dependence on His Word is crucial to Lutherans. We have described this necessity of the Word of God with the term *sola Scriptura*, meaning "Scripture alone." In chapters 2 and 3, we'll discuss the importance of Scripture alone as the beginning of our relationship with God and the foundation from which our life with God never leaves.

YOU GO FIRST

Those first words are awkward. Someone walks up toward you, smiling. That's a good sign, but only if that smile is for you. Don't smile back too much until you're sure someone else isn't behind you. Wait a moment, and if the smile continues, then it's for you. Now you're only five feet apart. You should say something, such as "Hello." But the timing is important. Who goes first? The one who walks up seems to be taking the initiative, and so maybe he should go first. But maybe you should say something to show you're interested. And so it ends up that you both say "Hello" at exactly the same moment. Then you both say, "You go first." And then, still in unison, "No, you go ahead." Finally, someone has to be first to say it again, alone: "Hello."

It isn't always clear who goes first. But with God, it's set from the beginning. He is the Father and we are His children. Like any parent, He goes first. Parents speak first to their newborn children. What a strange relationship it would be to have parents say nothing to their child, waiting for her to speak first. How could the parents ever hold in all that they want to say and all that their child needs to hear? Your baby daughter can't say "I love you" yet, but she can know it when you say it.

God also comes first to us, calling us into the relationship He has already planned for us. This calling is like the shepherd calling his sheep by name. Their relationship comes out through his voice and their names. Jesus describes His calling of His people in the same way in John 10:3–4: "The sheep hear his voice, and he calls his own sheep by name and leads them out. When he has brought out all his own, he goes before them, and the sheep follow him, for they know his voice." What a wonderful relationship of knowledge and trust. God speaks and creates that same trust with us through His Word.

The analogy of the sheep and shepherd points also to the action done first by the shepherd. Lost sheep can't summon the shepherd, but the searching shepherd calls his sheep.

> Lost sheep can't summon the shepherd, but the searching shepherd calls his sheep.

The feeble voice of the lamb fades within feet, but the shepherd's voice crests the hills and covers the valleys. In the same way, God takes the initiative to find endangered lambs even when they appear to be running from Him.

This first word by God happens repeatedly in the Scripture, often turning people from despair or destruction. For example, in 1 Kings 18, Elijah had a tremendous victory when fire came down from heaven to demonstrate the truth of God's power. But the next day, Elijah was depressed and frightened when Queen Jezebel threatened to kill him. He fled to the desert, where God had repeated conversations with him, beginning by asking, "What are you doing here, Elijah?" (1 Kings 19:9). God knew Elijah would complain of his lonely, dangerous life, but God patiently listened, spoke to him, and finally returned Elijah to his ministry.

Not only did God's Word turn Elijah from fear to confidence, but the Word of God can also turn a man from death to life. Saul was a Pharisee, determined to find and kill as many Christians as possible. Jesus spoke to him with the shattering words, "Saul, Saul, why are you persecuting Me?" (Acts 9:4). Saul, later called Paul, was incredulous at hearing this heavenly voice. However, Jesus identified Himself as the one Saul was persecuting. The stunning words of God began a new understanding and a courageous faith in the changed man, Paul.

The Word of God comes to us perhaps in some of these same situations. Maybe, like Saul, we are blind to what we are doing wrong, but God warns us before we are destroyed. Like a patient parent, God speaks through the muffler of our covered ears, breaking through to us by His strong Word. On the other hand, we might be the discouraged and frightened Elijah, complaining about how life has turned out. In our discouraged retreat, God seeks us, calls us by name, and restores us to His purpose for our lives.

It should be simple. In a relationship, you communicate. Text, email, call, or leave a message. All these can bring us the news we want to hear. Yet they can also all leave us asking, "What? What did you mean?" Sometimes you have to have someone else read it with you. Sometimes it's obvious. A text that starts, "You're a wonderful person and we can still be friends," doesn't need to go on. You know how it will end. However, other times you want some help understanding the message. What exactly does "You're the best!" mean?

Here's the good news. God's Word, on which our relationship with Him depends, is so clear that we don't need an interpreter. We can read it, understand it, and trust it immediately ourselves. That's the intention of God. When He says that He loves the world and has given us His Son to save the world, we understand John 3:16–17 and its wonderful verbs: *loved*, *gave*, and *saved*. This trust begins with the very nature of God Himself as the one who changes not and says only that which is eternally true.

Wasn't that one of the keys to understanding a message? What is the character of the person sending the message? Could you trust your seventh-grade friend who told you that you were her best, truest, and only real friend? With words such as that, you wanted to believe her. But you had this suspicion—and you were right—that you were the fifth person to whom she had said this. Get in line. You're not that special. That was the real message.

God is not a seventh grader tossing out promises that will never be kept. His Word is trustworthy because it is the nature of God to be true. We are drawn to God because of His nature. The promises of His truthful Word are many:

"The sum of Your word is truth" (Psalm 119:160); "I the LORD speak the truth; I declare what is right" (Isaiah 45:19); "For the law was given through Moses; grace and truth came through Jesus Christ" (John 1:17). God clearly promises to speak only the truth.

But everyone claims to speak the truth. Why believe these words? Because these words cost Him His life.

Why believe these words? Because these words cost Him His life.

These promises sent the Son of God to be tortured, nailed, and crucified. These promises are not promises of what we could gain if we could ever be perfect. They are the promises of God's love even while we are the worst sinners. Romans 5:7–8 makes this contrast between our actions and God's: "For one will scarcely die for a righteous person—though perhaps for a good person one would dare even to die—but God shows His love for us in that while we were still sinners, Christ died for us." The promises of God come without any worthiness in us. But God delivered His Son to death for us when we were still in the fullness of our sins. Therefore, since He has made such a promise and kept it, we can trust His Word.

Because His Word can be trusted, we don't need an interpreter. No one needs to be between us in this relationship. It might help to ask your best friend to interpret an ambiguous text: "You're wonderful, the best!" It's fine to ask for help—if she's impartial. But what if there's some jealousy or she just doesn't like him for some reason? Consider carefully what she says.

The Word of God needs no meddling by someone in the middle. God speaks to us clearly by His Son. Hebrews 1:1–2 makes this contrast: "Long ago, at many times and in many ways, God spoke to our fathers by the prophets, but in these last days He has spoken to us by His Son." In the words of Jesus, we hear the One who speaks clearly because He is one of us. He has taken on our flesh and lived among us. He has worked, walked, hungered, and died. He spoke in parables of the things we know: seeds and soil, rocks and weeds, lost coins and angry sons. Because He has so lived and known us, we can understand Him.

IT NEVER SOUNDED SO GOOD

When I was about seven years old, I visited my friend Larry's house, and his mother made the best peas ever. They were in a cream sauce, and I thought they were the most delicious vegetable ever put on a plate. So my mother called Larry's mother, asking for the magic recipe. It turns out they were simply frozen peas, cooked and served in milk. Nothing more. My mother assured me that she had made the same peas, the same way, and that hers tasted just the same. But somehow, they were different at Larry's house.

You've had those peas, haven't you? Somehow, the meal at your friend's house was just a little better. That first frozen pizza that you and your eighth-grade friend made was the best pizza ever. That first macaroni and cheese meal you made as a couple? You said you could eat that every night, and for the first three months, you pretty much did. The relationship makes the meal taste better than ever.

It's the same with words. The relationship changes the words. In the right relationship, words such as *friend*, *mine*, and *love* sound better than you've ever heard them. Now you know what those words mean, because finally they are attached to someone who is truly your friend. The relationship changes the words.

God's relationship with us changes the hearing of His Word. Lutherans believe that Scripture is divinely inspired; the Holy Spirit spoke the words through the men who wrote the Bible. In 2 Peter 1:21, we read, "For no prophecy was ever produced by the will of man, but men spoke from God as they were carried along by the Holy Spirit." Men spoke the words God gave them. This makes Scripture both familiar and new. It comes from men firmly grounded in our experience as they lived among us. But the words are also the very words given to them by the Spirit.

The words may not be new, but they carry more meaning and greater effect than we've ever experienced. Many might wish you peace, but that good wish only goes so far. It's different when Jesus says, "Peace I leave with you; My peace I give to you. Not as the world gives do I give to you. Let not your hearts be troubled, neither let them be afraid" (John 14:27). Jesus' words are that peace in themselves, and His words move us to His peace. We have heard these words before, but never with this effect. His words of forgiveness calm the troubled conscience; His words of power give courage to the frightened heart; His words of love convince us that we are not alone, for He is with us. You start a relationship by someone saying, "Hello." You might have said it many times before, but now, here, with the two of you, there really is a difference. So it is with God; His words are not like all the others we've heard. His Word sounds better and starts something altogether new.

FIRST-DATE FOOD

What would be good first-date food? I say, make it simple. Skip the lobster and anything with a name you can't pronounce. Even spaghetti can be a little too exciting. Chicken nuggets sound safe. That first date should be about looking into each other's eyes, not worrying about which fork to use.

The wonderful news of our start in God's relationship is that He meets us here through the lifelong ministry of Jesus. He lived among us and spoke in the simplest terms that we can understand. The parables tell the stories of seeds, weeds, and rocks, of runaway sheep and sons, and of a woman who wouldn't stop searching for a coin she had lost. We know all these stories because we've lived them. But then we discover that the story that is so well-known tells a new story, the story of our relationship with God. On a first date, the simplest meal of macaroni and cheese tastes better than it ever did before, all because of whom you are with. In the same way, the parables of Jesus and the clear words of the Bible are both familiar and more exciting than ever, because we find that we are with Him in His Word.

DISCUSSION QUESTIONS

1. Do you remember who said the first words to start an important relationship in your life? What did he or she say? How were those few words enough to start that relationship?

2. This chapter describes the words that God speaks first to start a relationship with us. Why does He need to go first in speaking to us?

3. Since God's Word is clear in itself, why do we study it and share our understanding of what He's saying?

4. In this chapter, I described the peas my friend's mother made. When have you had a meal that was better because of those who were with you? How are the words of God better because He says them to us?

5. Lutherans stress that God Himself speaks by inspiration through the Bible's words. Yet we also speak of the Bible in terms of the men—Moses, David, Matthew, Mark, and others—who wrote the Bible. What is the value of understanding the Bible as both the words of people like us and also the very words spoken by God?

6. This chapter's final section says that first-date food should be simple. Skip the lobster. Stick with chicken nuggets. How is the Bible also appealing because the promises of God deal with familiar essentials of life, such as forgiveness, peace, and love?

7. God won't be coming out with a new Bible anytime soon. Scripture is what we have. How can those sixty-six books of the Bible be enough to feed us for a lifetime and bring us to eternal life?

RESOURCES

For further study and understanding, please consult the following resources.

Luther's Small Catechism with Explanation (St. Louis: Concordia Publishing House, 2017). For an overview of reading God's Word, note especially pages 354–57.

"How to Read and Study the Holy Bible," in *The Lutheran Study Bible* (St. Louis: Concordia Publishing House, 2009), pages xxvi–xxx.

Lutheran Service Book, hymn 578: "Thy Strong Word."

CHAPTER 3

We Need to Talk

I once saw a young couple, John and Amy, sitting on a bench here at Concordia University Wisconsin. Amy was turned toward John, telling him something important. He stared at the wall with a glazed look. I sat down next to them and asked, "Did this conversation start with something such as this: 'We need to talk?'" Guardedly, they said yes. Turning to John, I said, "Here's what you do. The next time Amy says, 'We need to talk,' then right away you say, 'About how great I am and how lucky you are to be with me? You bet, let's talk!'" I thought it was a good line. John liked it, but Amy didn't look all that pleased.

That's because "We need to talk" is serious. It signals a new level in the relationship. You don't say that sentence on the first date. This is what you say after you've been together for a while. It says that we can be honest with each other and finally face some things that we've avoided. Now, it's time to talk.

That's where we go in understanding our relationship with God. We've begun with the firm foundation of His Word alone, words that He speaks to us first. Now in that relationship, it's time for us to go deeper and hear more. We're still people of *sola Scriptura*, depending on Scripture alone for our connection with God. As we read that Scripture and as we live it by faith, God's message grows in breadth and deepens in meaning.

Two broad divisions of the Bible give us these dimensions of breadth and depth. Lutherans have long spoken of Law and Gospel, the commands of God and the promises of God's mercy. These two headings, Law and Gospel, are the summary of all that God says. They give us a wonderful shorthand by which we can read and live God's message. These are words that are as familiar as the Golden Rule and as exciting as God saying that the angels in heaven celebrate when one, even you, is found and brought home (Luke 15:7, 10). It's a serious talk that God has with us, but it ends with the celebration that He has found us and brought us home to Himself. Let's talk about all that.

MAYBE YOU DON'T SEE IT, BUT I'VE GOT TO TELL YOU

I have long believed that when you see a man consistently doing foolish things, you're looking at a man with no friends. No real friends, at least. Real friends would see his mistakes and say to him, "Don't do that!" Real friends stand at the edge of the cliff and shout, "Stop!" It sounds harsh, but it will save your life.

God is a true friend. God can see over the distance and into the depth that blinds us.

> God can see over the distance
> and into the depth that blinds us.

He cares enough about us to say, "Stop! You're going over the edge!" Those words of warning and direction from

God are the Law. The Law is the first division of the Bible's message, bringing the clear directions of God that we are to follow. These words are His powerful directions for the rest of our lives. His commands are not just another line on our endless to-do list. They're the opportunity to live in the intersection of God and His people, following His path to the fullest.

This intersection of God and our lives starts as a safety barrier, a curb that protects us from ourselves and others. The Law brings the protecting words of our Father, guarding us in a dangerous world. It's the desire of every parent with little children. You want to go with your child and protect him, saying to the other children: "Be good to this boy. Don't steal from him. Don't lie about him. Don't hate him." The commands of God say the same to us and for us. "Don't steal from one another." "Don't lie about one another." "Don't envy someone else's things and hate him or her for having them." The directions of God's commands are a shield around us and our loved ones.

But sometimes we don't hear the commands of God and are going over the cliff of our selfishness. Then God shouts the sharpest warning. "Stop! Look what you're doing!" The commands of God are the bright, flashing lights of the state patrol car, and you know those lights are for you. God's commands have warned us of our wrong actions ever since Genesis 2:17, when God warned what would happen if Adam and Eve ate of the tree: "But of the tree of the knowledge of good and evil you shall not eat, for in the day that you eat of it you shall surely die." From that warning on, we've heard the alarm of God.

We might imagine that this is the end of the Law, a warning of our destruction. But God has a final step in the Law in which He gives directions for our life together with Him. These directions involve the striking words of Jesus in the Sermon on the Mount: "If anyone forces you to go one mile, go with him two miles. Give to the one who begs from you, and do not refuse the one who would borrow from you" (Matthew 5:41–42).

These are challenging words, but think of the alternative. If you only give to get the same back, you never leave where you are. You stay the same person. If you go only one mile so that you can turn around and easily go back, you end up only where you were. But if you go one mile and then keep going, that's an adventure. If you do go farther, like a runner who doesn't turn around but keeps running ahead, then you better know someone. There had better be someone you can call to pick you up when your energy is gone. Fortunately, we know Someone. On this mile-upon-mile run, Someone has already gone ahead of us. He gave without receiving back. He went ahead even to the cross, when He could have turned around and retreated to heaven. We go the extra mile, because we do know Someone who went much farther for us. Perhaps it is in that extra mile that we especially know a small measure of the much greater journey He made for us.

CAN YOU COME AND PICK ME UP?

It was a perfect summer morning, and I headed out on an eighteen-mile run. But just about nine miles from home, I twisted my ankle on a crack in the road. I thought I could tough it out, and so I turned for home at the next road. But all I could do was limp. Finally, six miles from home, I came to a house that let me call home. I caught our daughter Nicole: "Honey, could you come and pick me up? I won't make it home."

That's where we are when the Law is done with us. We finally admit that we're not going to make it home. Heaven is way too far for us. That's when God speaks to us through the other division of Scripture: the Gospel. The Gospel is the Good News of God's actions that save us. The Gospel centers on Jesus as God's Son, who lived a perfectly righteous life that is then counted as ours. His death on the cross is also credited to us, so that both the demand of keeping the Law and the penalty of our failure are satisfied. This is an exchange of our sins and His perfection; as Paul described it, "For our sake He made Him to be sin who knew no sin, so that in Him we might become the righteousness of God" (2 Corinthians 5:21).

This action does what we so often wish to do. Can I take away the pain for my friend, for my child, for my spouse? I wish I were the one who was hurting, and not you. But as much as we want to make this exchange, we can't. The pain destined for one always finds its mark and can never be called off course. The pain strikes our loved one with full force, so strong that it continues on to our heart also.

The pain strikes our loved one with full force, so strong that it continues on to our heart also.

But with God, we have that wonderful exchange by which He takes the penalty and pain of sin destined for us and places it on Himself. Nothing is left to strike us. This isn't just for those who are deserving, for no one is deserving. Who merits the death of God's Son? No one; however, as Paul says, God's gift is opposite of what we would do: "For one will scarcely die for a righteous person—though perhaps for a good person one would dare even to die—but God shows His love for us in that while we were still sinners, Christ died for us" (Romans 5:7–8). The fierce accounting for sin that should have come to me went to Him instead. The horrific death of the cross, and the forsakenness on that cross as the sins of the world separated Him from God the Father, should all have been mine. But He stood in its way and said, "This is Mine, not yours."

A few years ago, I did a morning chapel message at Concordia University Wisconsin. It was based on John 18:36, when Jesus said to Pilate, "My kingdom is not of this world." To strike the point home, I asked, "Where is Jesus' place? What could He claim as His spot?" I went from one seat to another in our very large chapel, trying several different views, each time telling a student, or even a professor, to slide over. "Move, that's my spot." In good humor, they did. In the same way, Jesus could have taken every good and comfortable place for Himself. But what did He take? Of what place did He say, "That's Mine"? He took the manger in the stable, the bench in the carpenter's shop, and finally the cross and the tomb. Always in His life He pointed to the cross and said, "That's My place; not yours, not ever. I'm doing this alone, all for you."

I KNEW IT FROM THE FIRST MOMENT

"This is the one." That's the line that starts many good relationships. You've heard it. Maybe you've said it. The moment you saw him or her, you knew. This is the one. The relationship was set before it began. You were as good as married. You just needed to find out her name.

God's relationship with us is that full and immediate choice by God of us. He has chosen us from eternity, but knows every detail of our lives when He makes that choice. He has full forgiveness of all our sins already won by the death of Christ on the cross. This is a relationship that's driven by God's choice. Paul described it this way: "For you did not receive the spirit of slavery to fall back into fear, but you have received the Spirit of adoption as sons, by whom we cry, 'Abba! Father!'" (Romans 8:15). In this adopted relationship, we are His completely by His choice, today and forever.

How many best friends do you have? How many best, best friends? How many really, really, best, best friends? Probably only thirteen-year-olds worry about these fine distinctions. Still, it would be nice to have something unique about your relationship. You're the only two who go fishing together or attend the book club. You two are the only ones who love old movies. Because this is your special relationship, don't invite someone else to come along. This time is yours alone. This is especially true when dating. Don't bring your roommate on the date. This is just for the two of you.

That is what makes the Gospel message so unique. We're in this wonderful relationship with God, who has created us and chosen us as His own. But we're not alone. He has the same love for every person who has ever lived, and that's just fine with us. This dynamic would never work in any other relationship. Imagine a new dating relationship in which you discover that every love letter, text, and email he sent to you was sent at the same time to every other woman on campus. Well, that's the end of that relationship.

But that message of God's love is the foundation of our relationship. It is because God loves the whole world that He sent His Son to die. In addition, it is because He loves the whole world that we know He loves us. He cannot say that He loves the world but then say to one of us, "But not you." His love for the whole world is the assurance that you are loved. That love covers all the sins that we alone know, that love listens to our midnight worries, and that love has planned our future. His love is spread but never thin. It is shared but never any less.

> His love is spread but never thin.
> It is shared but never any less.

WE SHOULD KEEP TALKING

Remember John and Amy, that young couple I talked about at the start of the chapter? I'm glad to say I didn't ruin their relationship. They are happily married today, with no end in sight. We all need at times the fearful sentence, "We need to talk." If we dare to do that, maybe it won't be too bad. In fact, we might even say, "We should talk like this more often." And so we do with God's Word. We need to talk by hearing His Law and Gospel every day. We need His warnings and His directions on our walk with Him. We especially need His forgiveness and His promises of peace, hope, and joy. We should keep talking about how wonderful He is, how good His gifts are to us, and how beloved we are. Let's keep talking.

The first dates are done, and you've made it through the simple meals. Cheeseburger and fries, chicken nuggets and a salad were no problem. But now it's time to get a bit more adventurous. Visit each other's homes, and you'll see something new. Ketchup on everything: fries, scrambled eggs, mashed potatoes, and even bacon. Really, ketchup on bacon? Now I've seen everything.

As our relationship with God grows, we are brought into His thoughts and ways. At first, it is a stunning message. The Law tells us that merely trying harder won't work. The Law is strong, black coffee with no cream or sugar. It starts the meal of God's message with a sharp warning. But then, when we are tongue-scorched and heartsore, God gives us only Gospel.

> But then, when we are tongue-scorched and heartsore, God gives us only Gospel.

It is the cool sweetness of God's free forgiveness. It comes completely free. It is God's own meal, unlike any we have made ourselves. It takes patience and trust to hear both Law and Gospel, but only through this combined recipe does God feed us as we need.

1. When someone says to you, "We need to talk," how do you feel? When has it turned out surprisingly well?

2. God speaks to us the warning words of a true friend. If we already know His warnings in our conscience, why does He still need to speak these words through the Law in the Bible?

3. The last section of this chapter talked of the times when you discovered that the person in your new relationship did things differently from what you had ever done. When has this happened to you?

4. How do the Law and Gospel strike us as both surprising and yet welcome? How can the Gospel message of forgiveness and love be both what we've always wanted and yet surprisingly new when we hear it?

5. One of the key images of this chapter is our adoption from eternity. Why is it a great comfort to us that before our birth, God chose us as His own?

6. One of the mysteries of the Gospel is the universal love of God that still satisfies us individually. We normally want an exclusive relationship, but in the Gospel, we hear that God loves the whole world just as He loves us. How can this love for all reassure us?

7. If we know the messages of Law and Gospel already, why keep talking with God every day?

RESOURCES

For further study and understanding, please consult the following resources.

Formula of Concord, Article V: "The Law and the Gospel," in *Concordia: The Lutheran Confessions*, second edition (St. Louis: Concordia Publishing House, 2006).

"Law and Gospel: Identifying God's Ways with Mankind," in *The Lutheran Study Bible* (St. Louis: Concordia Publishing House, 2009), pages xxxi–xxxii.

C. F. W. Walther, *Law and Gospel: How to Read and Apply the Bible* (St. Louis: Concordia Publishing House, 2010).

Lutheran Service Book, hymn 579: "The Law of God Is Good and Wise"; hymn 580: "The Gospel Shows the Father's Grace."

PART II

GRACE ALONE:

THE WONDERFUL REASON WE'RE TOGETHER

CHAPTER 4

Do You Want to Go Bowling?

Holly and I went bowling on our second date. There is nothing about us that says, "Bowling." I still wonder why I thought this was a good idea. I wonder even more why she said yes. The bowling lanes on our college campus cost a dollar a game, and so the whole evening shouted, "Cheap!" Also, neither of us has any bowling talent. I wonder if we even broke one hundred points—with both our scores combined. But we went, we threw gutter balls, and we laughed. At the end, we didn't say, "We should go bowling some more." But we did say, "We should get together again." Bowling was done. But we had just begun.

Bowling was done. But we had just begun.

Why go bowling on your second date? We didn't go bowling to go bowling. We've never had a bowling date since. You go bowling to get to know this other person. Anyone can sit through a movie. But throw two gutter balls in a row, and let's see what you're made of. If you can laugh at yourself, then we might have something. We weren't very graceful that night in our bowling, but we were full of grace toward each other.

That's the distinction we need in the relationship God has with us. If we're trying to impress God with our competitive score against everyone else, it won't work. But if we have a relationship full of grace, from Him to us, then we have something. That's the relationship God has with us, and it's the center of our second key idea. After we've learned of our relationship with God through Scripture alone, then it is time to appreciate that in this relationship, we're dependent on *sola gratia*, grace alone. Grace is God's wonderful motivation to call us His children, to declare that we are innocent in His sight, and to announce that we are the Bride and Christ is the Bridegroom. All this comes by grace alone.

THE NEW BEDSIDE TABLE

I grew up in an old farmhouse. One morning, I woke up to find a brand-new bedside table next to me. My parents had bought it for me as a surprise. I loved it. It was new, and it was mine. When Holly and I got married, it went with us on all our moves. When we settled in Butternut, Wisconsin, it ended up as the bedside table for our daughter Nicole. It's still with Nicole at her home in Denver. It's fifty years old, scratched and dented, but I am so glad to see it still in the family. It was perfect when it was new, and it's even better now that it's old.

It was perfect when it was new, and it's even better now that it's old.

We are the new and old creation of our Father, perfect when we were new and somehow even better in our relationship with Him now. That's all because of grace. We began with a new, perfect creation that reflected God. As Lutherans, we believe the dramatic words of Genesis when God said, "Let Us make man in Our image, after Our likeness" (Genesis 1:26). In that relationship, we were the faultless expression of God's love. We weren't just a factory-made table, but we were the personal product of God's own hands. God shaped the dust into the first man, Adam, and breathed into him the breath of life. He took the rib of Adam and from it made Eve (Genesis 2:7, 21–22). In that first creation, God's grace expressed Himself. While all creation points to God, we are the clearest mirror of Him.

When it was brand-new, my little table was perfect. But it didn't stay that way. Holly and I moved it seven times to the various apartments and houses we've had. Nicole then carried it to Denver. It's been around! But every scratch and water ring tells a story. In fact, that's the best part. Neither Holly nor Nicole saw it as just an old, scratched table. They knew the story that made it special to me. My mom and dad are gone, and I'm not that farm boy anymore, but the little table is still here.

We didn't last long in the perfection of Eden. In short order, as Genesis 3 tells us, Adam and Eve reached for the one fruit not to be eaten. That broke their perfection and sent Adam and Eve into hiding from God. They went from being the bright, full-length reflection of God to two people hiding in the deepest shadow. This was more than a simple scratch in their relationship. God had warned that in the day they ate of that fruit, they would die (Genesis 2:17). How easy it would have been for God to reject them from that day on. He could have started over and made new people.

But our relationship with God is not a brittle perfection. One scratch doesn't send Him away. In fact, it's the scars that hold us together. Our willful, rebellious sins aren't beauty marks in themselves. Any reasonable view of them, like that little scarred table, would reject us. But grace alone views those scars differently because of another set of scars. It's the scars of the cross of Jesus that speak of His grace, and it's the scars of Jesus that keep us in this relationship. We are far from Eden. But our Father looks not at our distance but at the scars of His Son. Isaiah spoke of it this way: "Upon Him was the chastisement that brought us peace, and with His wounds we are healed" (Isaiah 53:5). God chooses to see us next to the cross on which Jesus is found, "stricken, smitten by God, and afflicted" (Isaiah 53:4). His wounds are the marks of the grace that welcomes us.

> His wounds are the marks of
> the grace that welcomes us.

THE OLD DRESSER COMES TO LIFE

Much of the furniture in my room as a boy had come from someone else. The biggest piece was the four-drawer dresser that my Aunt Mae got for me. Mae saw the dresser being thrown away by a rich family in Minneapolis and rescued it for me. She and her husband, Howard, brought it up to our farm. Mae's kindness covered the cracked veneer and missing drawer handle. As you can guess, I had it growing up, and when we got married, it moved with us. It became our son Steve's dresser. Finally, about three years ago, it was done. All the veneer was cracked and more handles were missing. It was time to bring the dresser to the curb.

But that morning when I put it on the curb, I noticed that the drawer sides were not plywood, as I assumed, but beautiful, solid oak. I couldn't throw that oak away. Instead, I got out a saw and sawed the oak sides out. Now what to do with them? Since a dresser is a box of boxes, I decided to make several boxes from that oak. I made two for Steve and two for me. After all, for both of our boyhoods, that had been our dresser. Now the boxes could carry on the tradition. They turned out beautifully and should be in the family for another hundred years at least.

The rejected is rescued. That's grace again. Grace sees what's on the curb and brings it back in.

Grace sees what's on the curb and brings it back in.

And so God welcomes us into a relationship with Him by grace alone. The parable of the prodigal son, found in Luke 15, shows this welcome by grace. The father's son took the inheritance and ran to a far country, scattering the money as he went. When he was hungry and desperate, he returned to his father, expecting at best to become a servant. But the father welcomed him with clothes, ring, shoes, and a feast. He had done nothing to deserve any of this. But grace is not about deserving anything. Grace celebrates that the lost has been found. Grace is not an accountant's ledger. Grace is a party invitation.

Grace is not an accountant's ledger. Grace is a party invitation.

You are the rescued dresser, the priceless daughter or son. You may believe that you have no value to anyone and that you outlived your worthiness decades ago. Some may have put you on the curb and said, "Good riddance." But by grace alone, God welcomes us as His own. We are the adopted children, chosen by grace: "He chose us in Him before the foundation of the world, that we should be holy and blameless before Him. In love He predestined us for adoption to Himself as sons through Jesus Christ" (Ephesians 1:4–5). Because it is by His gracious choice, our relationship doesn't waver with each day's failure or success. By grace alone, God has chosen us into this relationship. God welcomes us as prodigal children with joyous, heavenly laughter. He has already placed our sins onto His Son on the cross, so He can wrap His arms around us and welcome us home.

TRY TO EXPLAIN THIS

A relationship standing on grace alone sounds wonderful. Nevertheless, we probably still have questions. The main question is this: "Why would God do this?" What's He getting for all this generosity? There has to be a reason for grace.

It's a bit like the day I got stopped for speeding. I ride a motorcycle the sixty miles round-trip to work almost every day, even during the Wisconsin winters. One January morning, it was fourteen degrees but the roads were clear, so I rode my Honda VFR. I was on Highway 57 as it merged onto Interstate 43. The four-lane Highway 57 includes a long stretch that functions as an on-ramp to the interstate. However, while the interstate has a speed limit of seventy miles per hour, the smaller highway has a speed limit of fifty-five miles per hour. I was in the right lane when a white Toyota Camry sedan passed me. Yes, I was going over the limit, but this fellow was going a good five to ten miles per hour faster than I was. He passed me but then pulled in front of me and slowed way down. Come on! Why pass me if you're going to die in front of me? Then I looked in my mirrors. They were all lit up with blue and red lights. The state patrol was coming up fast.

The Camry driver knew he was guilty and pulled onto the shoulder. I moved over too so the trooper could go around me to the Camry. However, the trooper pulled in behind me. Seeing that, the Camry took off and I was left. I stopped as the trooper pulled in behind me. The first question the trooper asked was, "Do you know how fast you were going?" Well, I didn't know exactly, but almost certainly over the limit. What I wanted to say, but didn't, was that the Camry was going much faster than I was. Why aren't you chasing him? He's your fugitive.

We all have a white Camry in our lives. The white Camry is the person who is clearly worse than we are. If God asks you, "Do you know how many commands you've broken?" don't you want to point to your white-Camry person and say, "Well, some, but not nearly as many as she has"? That would be the reason God should forgive us. We may be wrong, but we're not the worst. But in that case, forgiveness wouldn't be by grace. It would just be a comparison, a contest, and our security would rest on making sure we were slightly better than someone else. Somehow, we would rather be excused by comparison than forgiven by the cross.

Somehow, we would rather be excused by comparison than forgiven by the cross.

Grace insists that we drop all our comparisons.

Grace is also seen in the next question by the trooper. After asking how fast I was going, he asked, "Why were you going so fast?" I was going to work and it was fourteen degrees. That's not a bad excuse, but I wish I had had a better one. It would have started with, "Sir, you have to understand. I'm on my way to . . ." Insert here a great reason, something involving a hospital, a lost child, or a plane that's leaving in twenty minutes.

What do you think will work with God? When God asks why you were breaking all those commandments, you want to say, "I know it was wrong, but You have to understand . . ." Let me tell You all my good intentions. We want to explain, not confess, so that God sees that we aren't really out-and-out criminals. We've just been misunderstood.

Is that grace? Not even close. Grace is not a platform for excuses. Grace wasn't interested in hearing how and why the prodigal son wasted all the money. Grace doesn't ask what happened, because grace already knows. Grace doesn't live in a fiction of what might have been. Grace looks at what we actually did, for whatever reason we did it. Yet, knowing that, grace still welcomes us home.

But maybe that forgiveness is also looking ahead to the future. After the state trooper asked if I knew my speed and why I was going over the limit, he went back to the car. I waited by the bike. You pray a lot in that moment. He came back with only a warning. Slow down and get there safe. I think the fourteen degrees helped. Maybe he thought it best not to push my craziness with a ticket.

How do you drive away when you get a warning? Hands on the wheel, ten and two positions. Signals on, long look over your shoulder, creep up to just under the limit. Don't even think about that breakfast burrito that's sitting next to you. Officer, if you give me just a warning, I'll be good.

We've certainly tried that with God also. Is grace just a chance to be better? Is grace an empty slate on which we can write our promises? No, for two reasons. First, it wouldn't be grace but only a reasonable trade: forgiveness now for better behavior tomorrow. Also, we would never keep it up. How long are you going to behave after the warning? Admit it; you're eating that burrito before it gets cold. Our promises to God would never last. Grace is grace because we can't fully explain it. It is the reason for God's forgiveness, and that is His choice in light of His Son. We can't explain it, but we can believe His promises. Grace welcomes us home, and nothing more is needed.

SHOULD I REFINISH THE TABLE?

I'm riding my motorcycle to Denver next week to see our daughter Nicole and son-in-law Dan. The old bedside table will be there. Should I offer to strip the finish, sand it, stain it, and get three coats of varnish on it? No, I don't think so. It's old, and it's not really beautiful anymore. But it's been in the family for over fifty years, just the way it is. It doesn't need perfection. It's here by grace.

We are taken into the household of God by grace. We were never perfect, but God chose us as His own, adopted us as His children, and continues to welcome us home after every prodigal journey. Don't try to explain grace or measure up to its gifts. Simply hear His words of welcome and know it is all by grace alone.

A GRACE-FULL MEAL

You start your relationship by eating out, but the relationship moves ahead when you start cooking the meal yourself. This is a time of grace. You're just starting to know each other, but you don't know everything. Should you use organic tomatoes? How much garlic is too much? Should the bread be soft and easy to pull apart, or should it be crusty enough to break a tooth? No one will get all this right the first time.

Eating together takes grace. Eat everything on the table, ask for seconds, and say you want to have this exact meal again. Grace doesn't ask questions. Grace celebrates being together. God includes us in His grace and brings us to His banquet. It's not because we've contributed the perfect side dish. We have brought nothing, but He feeds us daily bread and celebrates when any of us is found at His table. Grace is His boundless invitation to come, no matter who we are. Grace reaches the most distant and unlikely guests and has the table ready when they come.

1. The chapter started with the second date of bowling. When have you done something completely outside your skills and yet it turned out well, maybe even starting a new relationship?

2. We have a relationship with God based on grace. Though grace is hard to define, how would you describe it?

3. Adam and Eve began with perfection but soon depended on grace alone for their relationship. What do we know about God only through grace?

4. The chapter described old furniture that has more love than looks. What furniture do you have that means more than any price you could get for it?

5. We are rarely attached to the scratched, the beaten, and the old. How do we find a grace-filled beauty in the scars and wounds of Jesus on the cross?

6. This chapter described the time I was stopped for speeding while the white Camry got away. Why are we so drawn to comparing ourselves against white-Camry types instead of depending on grace alone?

7. Forgiveness by grace alone doesn't need our excuses or explanations. Since all our usual defenses are gone, how can we trust that grace alone is God's motivation to forgive us?

RESOURCES

For further study and understanding, please consult the following resources.

Luther's Small Catechism with Explanation (St. Louis: Concordia Publishing House, 2017). See especially Luther's explanation of the Apostles' Creed, the First Article.

"God Is Three-in-One," in *The Lutheran Study Bible* (St. Louis: Concordia Publishing House, 2009), page 1815.

Lutheran Service Book, hymn 744: "Amazing Grace."

CHAPTER 5

We Have to Ask, "Why?"

In a growing relationship, there's a happy mystery. There's something you want to know, but you don't ask. The question is this: "Why are you with me?" There seems to be a secret here. "Why are you with me?" It can't be the car, the concert tickets, or the help fixing your computer. If that's why we're together, it won't be enough. Soon a faster car and a better concert will split us up.

Why is someone with you? Maybe you don't dare to ask, in case they ask themselves the same question. Maybe they don't have a good answer either. Or you don't ask the question because it sounds too pitiful, begging for a compliment. Instead, you wonder in silence and hope that whatever the reason, the two of you stay together.

The amazing thing about God is that He wants us to ask. "God, why are You with me?" We can't help but wonder, and so He invites us to ask. The answer certainly isn't in any quality in ourselves or any promise we'll make for the future. The answer is grace alone. Grace is God's wonderful motivation to declare us innocent, even in the face of our obvious sins. Grace is His firm hold on us. It's not our doing, but it's the living breath of our relationship. Our emphasis on grace alone will focus in this chapter on the work of Jesus as the Son of God and also true man. His life in human flesh is pure grace, and His standing in our place completes the Father's gracious choice of us. In addition to the Son, the Holy Spirit reassures us that the promises of God are true by grace alone. The Spirit not only speaks these promises to us convincingly but He also lives within us to bring those promises to life each day. By all the actions of the Trinity, we can dare to ask, "Why are You with me?"

> By all the actions of the Trinity, we can dare to ask, "Why are You with me?"

HE CAME TO STAY

Many college students work as counselors at summer camps. Let's say that you're one of them, and you started a new relationship this summer after your freshman year of college. You met Bob from North Dakota, and he's wonderful. But this relationship will only last until the end of August, when camp closes. Then everyone goes back home, and the promises of staying in touch will be summer leaves, blown away before Halloween.

But what if, without warning, Bob says, "I'll transfer colleges. I'll go to school at Concordia with you. That way, we can see each other every day." Wow, that is one serious step. You wouldn't have dared to ask for this. It's a little shocking. This puts some pressure on you! What if it doesn't work out? What if he finds out what you're really like at school? Now all your school friends are going to meet him—what will they think? Somehow, all these questions come to you at once as you say, "Good, ahh, that . . . that would be good." He says, "Don't worry. It will be good. It will be great."

And it was. This is the story of God in Christ. Jesus came to live with us in the closest way by God's grace. When Jesus became incarnate, He took on our human nature. He is both true God and true man at the same time. He didn't merely come to visit us, to make a summer relationship and leave us with nothing but memories and pressed dry flowers. As the Father chose to adopt us, so the fulfillment of that choice came through the Son. God does what we would never have imagined. He didn't merely choose us as His own, but He chose to take our human nature onto Himself. He chose to live with us where we already are.

The lasting wonder of the incarnation of Jesus is the center of Lutheran theology. Lutherans focus, as does the Bible, on the coming, arrival, life, death, and resurrection of Jesus above all. His life story is the greatest extent of God's relationship with us. When Jesus takes on the fullness of our flesh, then the barrier between God and us is broken. Paul expressed the union this way: "For in Him the whole fullness of deity dwells bodily" (Colossians 2:9). What a relationship He has chosen with us. By being true God and true man for all time, Jesus made an eternal bond with us. He didn't take off His human nature, but as He made clear when He showed His wounds from the cross to His disciples, He is true God and true man still today (John 20:20, 27). In my illustration with Bob, Bob is investing three years of college to make this relationship work out. But what is that compared to Jesus' willingness to dwell with us over thirty years on earth and to live forever as man and God? Our relationship with God succeeds because of His gracious incarnation.

I'LL CARRY THE LOAD

Tonight, we're going out to eat with friends in Sheboygan. It's our turn to pay. We try to keep track of this and get the check every other time. But it's hard with this couple, because they're so generous. They would pay fourteen times in a row if we let them. Then, if we did finally pay, they would thank us so much, as if we had paid every time. So, tonight it's our turn to pay.

That's how relationships work, at least most of the time. It's your turn to pay, your turn to decide where we go, and your turn to choose the movie. We learn early in life that you have to take turns. But in our relationship with God through the incarnation of Jesus, it is all pure grace alone. A grace-alone relationship doesn't go back and forth between His turn and then ours. We don't live in fear of a bill coming that we can't handle. We don't worry that there's a cost that will end our relationship. He snatches up the bill with a nail-scarred hand and says, "I've got this."

> He snatches up the bill
> with a nail-scarred hand
> and says, "I've got this."

Paul describes His payment in Ephesians: "In Him we have redemption through His blood, the forgiveness of our trespasses, according to the riches of His grace, which He lavished upon us, in all wisdom and insight" (Ephesians 1:7–8). Martin Luther expressed Jesus' willingness to pay this cost this way: "[He] has redeemed me, a lost and condemned creature, purchased and won me from all sins, from death, and from the power of the devil; not with gold or silver, but with His holy, precious blood and with His innocent suffering and death" (Small Catechism, the Creed, Second Article).

It's breathtaking when we begin to realize the expense He paid to make us His own. The cruel death on the cross, during which He suffered the penalty of all our sins, is a price we can barely grasp. He made this payment without any expectation on our part. Who are we to tell God to allow His Son to die for our debts? What relationship do we have with God that would compel Him to die under the whole load of our sins? We could never imagine this price, nor demand its payment.

Now that payment of His incarnate death and the wonder of His resurrection from the dead stand entirely in our place. Remember Bob, who is willing to move from North Dakota to be with you? Bob does all the moving. He isn't suggesting that you meet halfway in Minneapolis. No, he's coming the whole way, paying all the cost, to be with you. In the same way, and even more, Christ's payment of death is graciously accounted by God as the entire payment needed for us. Paul writes, "For by grace you have been saved through faith. And this is not your own doing; it is the gift of God, not a result of works, so that no one may boast" (Ephesians 2:8–9). God accounts this death as equal to the required death of all people, since this is His Son. The value of His death stands as equal to every penalty that we owe. Jesus comes in human flesh, from the manger to the cross, to remove every barrier in our relationship with God. All this, without a single bill to us, is by grace alone.

Billy has never really had a friend. At least, he hasn't had a friend who would promise to come tomorrow and then actually come. He's had disappointments, but not friends. Then Noah and his family moved into the neighborhood at the start of summer. By mid-July, Billy had hope. Noah came over at least three afternoons a week. Then, today, he said he was going to put up a tent in his yard tomorrow and sleep in it overnight. Best of all, Noah said Billy should come over, help put up the tent, and then camp with him that night in the yard. This is the best offer Billy has ever had.

But will it happen? Billy starts to remember all the promises others made and how none of them turned out. He waited by the window, but no one came. Maybe Noah is no different. Billy is about ready to start unpacking his backpack. Better to be safe at home than disappointed down the street.

Billy needs a mom. He needs a mom who has already called Noah's mom to make sure this is really happening. It is. Noah's mom is excited about the boys' big adventure and is actually thankful that Billy will come. So when Billy's mom sees him emptying his backpack, she says, "Hold on! You're going to need that. I just talked to Noah's mom. You boys are camping tonight. Pack up and get ready."

We are Billy. We have this wonderful news about the grace of God that chose us as the Father's own and the grace that sent His Son to be born in our flesh. We are promised not a night in a tent but an eternity in His heaven. We have this all by the promises of the Bible, and it's the best news we could imagine. But we can't believe it. It's too good, beyond anything we've ever seen. It can't be true.

But it is true. It is beyond us, and we can't believe it. Luther's Small Catechism says, "I believe that I cannot by my own reason or strength believe in Jesus Christ, my Lord, or come to Him" (Small Catechism, the Creed, Third Article). Paul described the limitations of our natural understanding, saying, "The natural person does not accept the things of the Spirit of God, for they are folly to him, and he is not able to understand them because they are spiritually discerned" (1 Corinthians 2:14). Our disappointment with our own promises, coupled with the mystery of Jesus being true God and true man, means we can't grasp the Gospel's promise of free forgiveness. Broken promises we know, but a God who keeps His impossible promise, who lives with us but without our sin—He is beyond us.

This relationship needs the Holy Spirit to convince us that these promises are true. The Small Catechism continues from our previous quote about our inability to believe, saying, "But the Holy Spirit has called me by the Gospel, enlightened me with His gifts, sanctified and kept me in the true faith" (Small Catechism, the Creed, Third Article). This makes all the difference when we hear the promises of the Gospel. Paul contrasts our doubt and faith this way: "For the word of the cross is folly to those who are perishing, but to us who are being saved it is the power of God" (1 Corinthians 1:18). Now we believe by the power of the Holy Spirit, who recalls those promises for us and brings faith to believe them.

Billy's mom knows how this night of camping is going to happen. You don't trust two seven-year-olds to plan this. Similarly, the Spirit recalls for us the teaching of Jesus, stressing within us the words of forgiveness, hope, and promise that we need each day. Jesus described this work of the Spirit this way: "The Helper, the Holy Spirit, whom the Father will send in My name, He will teach you all things and bring to your remembrance all that I have said to you" (John 14:26). We need this repetition of even the best news of the Gospel, because it is news that exceeds all we've known. So the Spirit speaks Jesus' words to us, strengthening our faith to trust those promises.

To do this work of reminding us, the Spirit lives with us. Should Billy's mom walk with Billy the block and a half to Noah's place? I think so. Walk together and talk about what a great night it will be. In the same way, the Holy Spirit doesn't send us away alone but goes with us every step. Jesus said, "And I will ask the Father, and He will give you another Helper, to be with you forever, even the Spirit of Truth. . . . You know Him, for He dwells with you and will be in you" (John 14:16–17). The Spirit graciously accompanies us and speaks to the Father on our behalf (Romans 8:26). Billy's mom assures Billy it will be all right, and then she asks Noah's mom to watch over Billy through the night. The Spirit does the same for us. He walks each day with us as we approach our Father's home. He speaks to the Father ahead of us so that our way will be protected and the door opened. He speaks to the Father for us even as He repeats the Father's words to us.

> He speaks to the Father for us even as He repeats the Father's words to us.

All this is the pure grace of God in love for us. What kindness God has shown by His grace in this relationship!

It is all His gift of choice and mercy. Because of that, our relationship that stands on grace alone has no fear. God has made every sacrifice for us so that we can know Him and trust in Him by grace alone.

THERE'S NO RUSH

The best meals take time. A good meal at your favorite restaurant means you put away the phone and your watch. Don't worry about how long it takes for the meal to come. Order dessert and get the drinks refilled. No one's hinting that we go, so let's stay. After all, it's not the food that keeps you there. It's the joy of eating together and discovering that the other person is just as glad to stay as you are.

That's the joy of the incarnation of Jesus. He came to be with us forever. He is Immanuel, the God who is with us. He is the incarnate God who is also forever true man, and He promises He will never leave us. He didn't come to visit; He came to stay. It's His joy and ours that we share each moment, every meal and day together. There's no rush. Neither He nor we are leaving.

1. Have you ever asked someone, "Why are you with me?" How did that turn out for you?

2. On the other hand, why would God welcome that question, "God, why do You want to be with me?" What will we learn about God and His grace when we ask that question?

3. In this chapter, Bob volunteered to transfer colleges in order to build the relationship with you. While this is quite a step for Bob, how is the incarnation of Jesus to be both true God and true man much greater in terms of His sacrifice, and what it will bring to our relationship?

4. The Bible tells us about the incarnation of Jesus as true God and true man, but it remains amazing to us. What is almost unbelievable to us in the incarnation? Consider, for example, the eternal God being born of a virgin, the ever-living God choosing to die, and the holy God being credited with the sins of the world.

5. I trust that you felt for Billy and his slim hope that he finally had a friend in Noah. For all the plans the boys made, how did they still need their moms? For all our spiritual hope, why do we need the help of the Spirit?

6. What words of Jesus do you especially need to be reminded of by the power of the Spirit?

7. Our theme in this chapter has been the grace of God. How do the incarnation of Jesus and the presence of the Spirit express the gracious heart of God and His overflowing generosity and mercy?

For further study and understanding, please consult the following resources.

Luther's Small Catechism with Explanation (St. Louis: Concordia Publishing House, 2017). See especially Luther's explanation of the Apostles' Creed, the Second and Third Articles.

Formula of Concord, Article VIII: "The Person of Christ," in *Concordia: The Lutheran Confessions*, second edition (St. Louis: Concordia Publishing House, 2006).

"God Is Three-in-One," in *The Lutheran Study Bible* (St. Louis: Concordia Publishing House, 2009), page 1815.

Lutheran Service Book, hymn 575: "My Hope Is Built on Nothing Less."

PART III

FAITH ALONE:
BUILD THE TRUST

CHAPTER 6

GOD'S GIFTS BUILD OUR TRUST

You have to ask. If you don't ask, your mother is going to ask. You're in a new relationship, and it's all going well. You've made it through the first date movie, the second date of bowling, and the third date when you dared to eat spaghetti, complete with the tomato stain on your shirt. But it's going well. You talk almost every day and plan almost every event together. You even met each other's families, and everyone seemed normal.

But where is this relationship going? Your mother and best friend both want to know. Should you just ask straight-out? "We need to talk. Where is this all going?" That might be a little blunt. Wouldn't it be better if you didn't have to ask at all? What if you just knew that this was the relationship you've been waiting for? Wouldn't you love to know from the start that this is the one?

That's the relationship God has with us. It's going somewhere, and we know it. We've come to know the Trinity of Father, Son, and Holy Spirit. We know God through His reliable Word alone, and we know that the center of this relationship is His grace alone. We know that the Father has chosen to adopt us, and this without us deserving any of it. The Son has paid our entire debt of sin, becoming that sin itself through His death on the cross. By His incarnation, He came to live with us forever. We believe that almost unbelievable mercy through the Holy Spirit, who reassures us that these promises are true. All this is God's action, not our imagination. We know how this relationship is going, because He has made Himself known to us.

But where is the relationship going? It's going to a life such as we have never known. That's our short answer. Jesus makes it clear when He says, "I came that they may have life and have it abundantly" (John 10:10). It all comes through faith in the message of the Word; as John wrote, "These are written so that you may believe that Jesus is the Christ, the Son of God, and that by believing you may have life in His name" (John 20:31). We have the Word that tells of His grace. This combination of Word alone and grace alone then leads us to the third key, faith alone, *sola fide*. By faith alone, we hear God's promises and trust them. With that faith, we have the answer to our question: Where is this relationship going? By faith, it's going just where He promised: life today and endless life to come.

> Where is this relationship going? By faith, it's going just where He promised: life today and endless life to come.

To live on these promises of God takes faith alone. But we aren't in a blind faith. We have proof in the actions of God for us. In this chapter, we'll look carefully at the Means of Grace, which God uses both to create faith and to strengthen that faith. Baptism is God's once-in-a-lifetime act that unites our lives with His. Then the Lord's Supper, which we take frequently, directs us to the cross of Jesus as the ultimate work of God and proof of His love. With these two gifts of God, we have the evidence of God's love for us. Go ahead and ask us where this relationship is going. We'll point to Baptism and the Lord's Supper and say, "See how He loves us! Here God is with us, and forever we will be with Him."

I KNEW IT FROM THE START

You wish you did know from the start. Wouldn't it be great if the moment you walked into the job interview, you knew you had the job and that you'd love it? Wouldn't it be good if from the first minute of a class, you knew that you would actually enjoy this class and would do well in it?

Wouldn't it be good to know that it's all going well with you and God, right from the beginning? The gift of Baptism is our introduction to God's grace and is our assurance from God that our relationship is in His secure and loving hands. Lutherans see Baptism and the Lord's Supper primarily as God's gift to us. They are His actions done with and for us. The action of God initiates these gifts so that His promises bring the gifts that are in each. We have the relationship with Him as adopted children, already secure, through the washing of Baptism and the inclusion of our life with His.

This emphasis on God's actions received by faith is at the heart of the actions of Baptism. Baptism might be first understood as the washing that God does with us. The Greek word *baptizo* is generally used for washing, such as in Mark

7:4 with the washing of hands, cups, pots, and other vessels. When this verb is used of Baptism, it is a spiritual washing. Ananias said to Paul, "Rise and be baptized and wash away your sins, calling on His name" (Acts 22:16). In Baptism, God washes us not from an outward spot but from the deepest, inner stain of sin. His washing sees all our sins, those that we have tried to hide from ourselves and those we cannot reach. We can't stretch far enough back in the past to scrub sins away, and we can't go forward to the sins we haven't yet done. But God's complete washing in Baptism cleans every day of our lives.

When God has so cleansed us, He finds no fault with us. Paul describes this in terms of a wedding: Christ, "having cleansed her by the washing of water with the word, so that He might present the church to Himself in splendor, without spot or wrinkle or any such thing, that she might be holy and without blemish" (Ephesians 5:26–27). This washing both begins our relationship and endures throughout our days. Brides look magnificent on their wedding day but rarely, if ever, wear that dress again. Let the wedding pictures retell the story. But God sees us in the perfection of His washing every day. He doesn't see us in a yellowing dress that no longer fits. By faith, we hear Him say, "You are perfect in My sight."

> He doesn't see us in a yellowing dress that no longer fits. By faith, we hear Him say, "You are perfect in My sight."

Of course, it takes faith to believe this promise. Many weddings start late because the bride isn't perfect in her own eyes. Her mother and the maid of honor assure her that she looks great. Still she stands in front of the mirror saying, "I'm not sure." Left to ourselves, we would be the same in preparing to meet God. We would take forever, trying to look perfect at best but presentable at least. It takes faith to leave the mirror and walk down the aisle. It takes faith for us to stop looking at ourselves and to trust the promises of God. This trust is expressed beautifully in the Small Catechism, which asks, "How can water do such great things? Certainly not just water, but the word of God in and with the water does these things, along with the faith which trusts this word of God in the water" (Baptism, Third Part). The baptismal font is a reflecting pool. It doesn't reflect us, so don't waste time looking. No, the water of Baptism reflects God and His heavenly promises. Faith, which comes with these promises of God, allows Baptism to do its cleansing work.

WHEN DO YOU GET TO SAY "WE"?

It's more than grammar, going from third person singular to first person plural. You know your friendship is moving ahead when you start saying "we" and "us" and "ours." Those wonderful words are the change from the separate "she and I" to the much-better "we." If this relationship is going someplace, it's going to bring the two of us to "we."

Baptism does just this. It is the joining of lives together through the words and promises of God. When we're baptized in the name of the Father, Son, and Holy Spirit, our life is joined with the name and life of God. This means we're no longer strangers and aliens to God; rather, we are His own people. In fact, we've put Him on. Paul describes the union this way: "For as many of you as were baptized into Christ have put on Christ" (Galatians 3:27). Not only has God cleansed our lives, but He has also folded us into the life of His Son. By Baptism, He has brought us into the family with all the blessings that come through the Son.

When you had a wonderful friend growing up, didn't you want to be a part of their family? You even hoped they would invite you to go on vacation with them. But no, that wasn't going to happen. You can visit, but trips such as that are for family. But with Baptism's gifts, we are in the family. We don't have to hear of heaven, knowing we won't be in it. Instead, Jesus said, "In My Father's house are many rooms. If it were not so, would I have told you that I go to prepare a place for you? And if I go and prepare a place for you, I will come again and will take you to Myself, that where I am you may be also" (John 14:2–3). If you're asking where this relationship is going, then look by faith to the promise of the Carpenter. He is preparing now the rooms in which we will be with Him. This relationship is going someplace that lasts.

This relationship is going someplace that lasts.

IT'S TIME TO EAT

I bet you have this rule at your house: no cell phones at the table. No laptops, no tablets, and no remote controls, because at this table, we watch only our manners and one another. When it's time to eat, it's time to talk.

Maybe you go to a special place to make your meal extra special. It's the picnic table at the state park or the back booth at McDonald's. It's the restaurant that's famous for good food and slow service. Perfect. You don't want to hurry anyway. Let's relax and eat and talk, because we're a family.

That is the heart of the other Means of Grace that assures us of our relationship with God. Besides Baptism, we have the Lord's Supper as God's repeated assurance that we are His and that the key in our relationship, forgiveness, has been paid for by the very body and blood of Jesus. In this meal, we have the reassurance upon which our faith feeds. God gives us the body and blood of His Son so that we trust His promises and live already as His family. We come to His meal to receive His words and the bread, which is also His body. We share His meal because we're His family.

At the Lord's Supper, we hear some of the most important words Jesus said. They are simple words that we know by heart. He gave them bread and said, "'Take, eat; this is My body.' And He took a cup, and when He had given thanks He gave it to them, saying, 'Drink of it, all of you, for this is My blood of the covenant, which is poured out for many for the forgiveness of sins'" (Matthew 26:26–28). This bread and wine are more than just a meal. By these words, we have also the very body and blood of Jesus. Lutherans hold strongly to the simple clarity of these words, "This is My body." As Jesus is true God and true man in one undivided person, so also in this meal He gives us both the physical bread of the meal and also—in, with, and under the bread—He gives us His own body. Certainly, this is a deep truth, much like His own incarnation as God and man. Therefore, we take these words by faith as His promise and trust them just as we trust that He is both truly God and truly man.

Order someone a new car for her birthday. Put it in the driveway on her birthday morning. What a gift! But is it a gift, or does it still have to be paid for? If you made only this month's payment as well as title, tax, and license, and she has to pay for the next fifty-nine months, it's not a gift. It's a beautiful burden. Instead, show her the canceled check that paid the whole price. Now it's a gift.

The Lord's Supper is the canceled check.

The Lord's Supper is the canceled check.

In His body and blood, we have the payment made for our sins, just as He said, "This is My blood of the covenant, which is poured out for many for the forgiveness of sins" (Matthew 26:28). This very body and blood are that which have paid for our forgiveness. Paul says pointedly that Jesus lived "to reconcile to Himself all things, whether on earth or in heaven, making peace by the blood of His cross" (Colossians 1:20). In the Lord's Supper, we are invited to take, to eat and drink the body and blood that purchased our forgiveness. We don't doubt the news of this forgiveness; rather, we cherish the meal that reminds us of that payment and gives us that faith-building body and blood within us.

This memory takes faith, of course. It took faith to see Jesus was the Son of God even when He hung on the cross. It takes faith to believe that in His death, we have the value of the death of God's own Son. The death of the only Son of God is what pays for our forgiveness. It takes God's own gift of faith to believe that this bread and wine are more than a small meal. Faith in His Word makes this food more than a memory. It is receiving the body and blood, which have paid for our lives.

With that very body and blood comes the memory of all that He did. As Jesus instructed, we take the Supper in remembrance of Him (Luke 22:19). Our brief time at the altar rail can barely start our memories. But each time we commune, we can bring to mind a different healing, another parable, new words of forgiveness, and another defense of those in need. We take a walk through the Gospels with every setting of the Supper.

While we go back in memory, He comes forward to us in body and blood. The wonder of this meal is that here is the very body and blood of Jesus in, with, and under the bread and wine. They're not at a distance but in our hands. Yet, there's no fear in His nearness. We might have fled from such closeness with God. After all, we caused His broken death. Instead, He fills us not with dread of death but with life from His presence.

He fills us not with dread of death but with life from His presence.

He comes to connect with us as the branches connect to the vine, and so He brings out new life in us (John 15:5).

With the true body and blood of Jesus, graciously given for us to eat and drink, we know how this relationship is going. We don't have to invent our hopes. With the Lord's Supper, we hear His lasting words of forgiveness and we have the body and blood given individually to each one of us. We do more than hope that God has kindly seen us from heaven. He has pressed His body and blood into our hands and has spoken to us the words of forgiveness that He won for all. We know how this relationship is going.

WE NEED A MEAL, NOT JUST A PICTURE

By now, your relationship with each other has gotten serious. You see each other and eat together every day. That's good, as long as you have real meals. Cookbooks and websites have wonderful pictures of meals, but you need actual food. Photos are great as a promise of what's to come, but you're hungry and need a real meal, not a picture.

In our relationship with God, we have just such a meal. In the Lord's Supper, we have the actual meal of bread and wine. But with these we also have the body and blood of Jesus in, with, and under the bread and wine. Jesus said to eat this meal in remembrance of Him, so it's a time of remembering all that He did for us. But it is more than a perfect picture. It is the meal that strengthens our faith and unites us as His Body, the Church. It is the very body and blood that were broken and poured out for us to pay for our sins and to strengthen our bond with Him. This is the meal that is more than a picture.

1. How soon do you begin to wonder where a new relationship is going? Can you just relax and enjoy the relationship without wondering about its future?

2. Baptism is, at heart, a washing and cleansing. Consider images of forgiveness as a cleansing, such as Psalm 51:2: "Wash me thoroughly from my iniquity, and cleanse me from my sin!" Why is washing such an appropriate image of forgiveness?

3. Baptism gives us wonderful promises of cleansing, being clothed in Christ, and being included into the family of God. How do these promises also require faith?

4. Do you have a mealtime during which cell phones, tablets, and computers are not allowed? What good things happen when you put those away and talk? How is the Lord's Supper that time for the family of God?

5. The Lord's Supper gives us the body and blood of Jesus, and with it we remember the payment for our sins made by His death. What reassurance of our forgiveness comes by having His true body and blood in the Supper?

6. The Lord's Supper is done in memory of Jesus' ministry and words. What miracles, teaching, and acts of Jesus come to mind, especially when you take the Lord's Supper?

7. We started the chapter with the question about how the relationship is going. How is your relationship going with God? What assurances do you have in Baptism and the Lord's Supper?

For further study and understanding, please consult the following resources.

Luther's Small Catechism with Explanation (St. Louis: Concordia Publishing House, 2017). See especially Luther's explanation of the Sacrament of Holy Baptism and the Sacrament of the Altar.

Formula of Concord, Article VII: "The Holy Supper of Christ," in *Concordia: The Lutheran Confessions*, second edition (St. Louis: Concordia Publishing House, 2006).

"Baptized into Christ" and "Preparing for the Lord's Supper," in *The Lutheran Study Bible* (St. Louis: Concordia Publishing House, 2009), pages 1920, 1965.

Lutheran Service Book, hymn 601: "All Who Believe and Are Baptized," and hymn 720: "We Walk by Faith and Not by Sight."

CHAPTER 7

God Has an Everyday Place for Each of Us

You know your relationship is going really well when one of you says, "Can we do this for the rest of our lives?" This is more than just a perfect date or that thirtieth wedding anniversary vacation to Hawaii. Those are good times too, but it's really wonderful when an ordinary day together that ends with macaroni and cheese leaves you saying, "Can we do this forever?"

In Baptism and the Lord's Supper, we have high-point moments in our relationship with God. Those are moments we never want to change. Let's not leave the baptismal font, with its sparkling water and the words of our washing. Let's stay at the altar rail, with the Lord's Supper assuring us of forgiveness through His body and blood.

But we can't be at the font or altar all day. We have more to our life with God, more places to be, and more to do together. We have our worship and our vocation. In this chapter, we'll look at worship as that which we can do weekly and even daily to express the relationship God has with us. We'll also look at our vocation, the everyday work that expresses our trust in God and His plans for us. Through faith, we can see that our work is a way to do God's work for the benefit of the world. The good news is that worship and our vocation happen every day. Yes, we can do this for the rest of our lives.

LET'S GO HOME

When do you say, "Let's go home"? Maybe when the meal was undercooked and overpriced, when the extra butter on the popcorn didn't redeem the movie, or when the kids were hitting one another even before you got in the minivan. "Let's go home." We might not be doing very well right now, but we'll be better when we go home. There's food we can trust, and everyone has his or her own place to sit. When things haven't gone according to plan and we show it, let's go home.

> When things haven't gone
> according to plan and we
> show it, let's go home.

Worship is our home with the family of God. We'll speak of our weekly worship; for convenience, let's say Sunday morning, though we can worship every day of the week. But on Sunday morning, we find our place with the family of God, sharing the relationship that God has with us. There is a real place to fill. You may have that place picked out already, the pew where you always sit. Growing up, I knew we would always sit in the same pew, on the right side, halfway down the aisle, near the window for the breeze, but not where the sun would hit us. We had our place, and we trusted that everyone else knew it. If you want to get a Lutheran emotionally charged at the start of church, just sit in his place.

But worship with the family of God is more than the pew on the right side. It's sharing the common experiences that brought us into this relationship with God. Many congregations have the baptismal font at the entrance to remind us that we entered our relationship with God through His gift of Baptism. Once we're seated and worship begins, we find our place in the familiar liturgy, which is primarily God's gifts coming to us, and then our response of thanks. We continue that reminder of Baptism with the Invocation of the names of the Father, Son, and Holy Spirit. We confess our sins and hear the reassurance of forgiveness through the Absolution. We sing or speak that thanks with the words of a psalm and then, hungry for more of the Word, we hear the readings of Old and New Testament. The Gospel reading brings us to our feet in respect for the Savior. We sing again in thanks for what we've heard and in preparation for the sermon to come.

In the sermon, we hear the message of Law and Gospel. The sharp Law prepares us to hear the comforting Gospel. The news of free forgiveness energizes us to live new lives in the coming week. While not every Lutheran sermon follows the three-part pattern of Law-Gospel-sanctification, we look for the rhythm of God's Word. It reminds us of our need, assures us of His forgiveness, and points us to our new life together.

Following the sermon, we often sing the words of Psalm 51, asking that God would create in us a clean heart and renew a right spirit within us. With that psalm comes the Offering, as a way to express our thanks. After the Offering, we might end with our prayers, the Lord's Prayer, and a final Benediction. But most often we have the Lord's Supper as the final high point of the service. This is a time for us to remember especially that we're part of the much larger family of the whole Church. We're with fellow believers around the world as well as with those believers who have gone to heaven already. We sing with "angels and archangels and all the company of heaven" (*LSB*, Proper Preface). If you're looking for something to do with others forever, you have found it here.

We eat together the Supper while we also sing our thanks to God for this gift. We say a final prayer and hear the Benediction of God's blessing and peace. Then we walk out together. Perhaps we go on to another familiar place, such as the line for coffee and doughnuts or the Bible study that goes on between the services. Maybe we stand in the corner talking with the same friends every Sunday. But we're not closed off. We would be glad to have someone new step into our circle. Come on in, hear His Word, and receive His gifts with us.

Of course, it takes faith to enter into the church and to receive those gifts. With any spiritual modesty, we know that we've got no business being in God's presence. Nevertheless, we come with the same request that the tax collector had in Jesus' parable: "God, be merciful to me, a sinner" (Luke 18:13). Led by the Holy Spirit, we enter His house, say those words of confession, and stay to believe the promises of forgiveness that He gives.

The gift of faith lets us worship in truth with God and share that truth with others. We're the family that shares one faith. We're here because together we hear His Word calling us. We might have our own pews, and please, let us stay in our favorite pews and not have to move to the front. But each in our places, we share this faith. Ephesians 4:4–6 says it well: "There is one body and one Spirit—just as you were called to the one hope that belongs to your call—one Lord, one faith, one baptism, one God and Father of all." When we worship, we've come home.

DAD, LET ME! I CAN DO IT!

Worship brings us together as a family. Usually we think of that happening on Sunday, though we can certainly worship any day of the week. Daily, we can remember our Baptism, read God's Word, sing, and pray. We might do that privately or share some of that with our family or friends. It can become the heart of every day.

But it likely won't take all day. The largest share of the day is our work. At first, that sounds like a tug-of-war between our worship and the mundane parts of our lives. However, work is not the enemy of our spiritual life. In fact, work becomes another expression of the relationship that God has with us. In our work, God not only shows His loving care for us, but He also expresses His relationship with others. This is our Lutheran understanding of vocation.

When you were growing up, what work did you want to do? It was probably something that showed you weren't just a kid anymore. You wanted to mow the lawn with the power mower. You said that you could make the birthday cake for Dad. When you were sixteen, you volunteered to drive to the store and get five different things, not even needing to write them down.

I hope that you did some of those things with your dad or mom. You painted the whole house together that one summer. You tilled up a new garden together and picked a thousand weeds and rocks. You and your mother planned your sister's whole wedding, even making the wedding cake yourselves. After a long day in the fields, my very quiet father would only say, "We did good today." Maybe your parents were more talkative than my dad. Even so, it was still enough to hear him say, "We did good today."

It was still enough to hear him say, "We did good today."

Our Lutheran understanding of vocation sees our work as this sharing between our Father and ourselves. Your vocation expresses God's relationship with you throughout the nine-to-five of every day. Every vocation has equal value, because every honest vocation expresses the same gracious relationship with God. No single profession has greater worth, since they're all founded on His grace alone. The surgeon is no more valuable to God than the nurse, or the custodian, or the woman who files your insurance. Take any one of them away, and very soon you'll have no health care. The same goes for your loaf of bread. The farmer and his seed, the harvester with his combine, the trucker, the miller, and the baker at the deli—we need them all. God feeds us daily bread through every one of them.

This equality of the value of work also means that we each can express God's relationship with the world. We can wear the mask of God—for Lutherans, this is a popular way of expressing this truth. God allows us to do the work that He wants done. You remember how exciting it was when you finally got to do the job that your mom or dad usually did. You chose the Christmas tree and cut it down, dragging it out of the tree lot. You wrapped the Christmas presents yourself. You frosted the Christmas cookies. That wasn't work. That was growing up. Your dad and mom watched you and said, "You did a really good job." God allows us to care for His people, to feed them, heal them, teach them, and guard them. All that is His kindness, and He lets us show it.

We take this all by faith. There are some Monday mornings that your work doesn't feel divine. There are people who have no idea that what you do matters to them or anyone else. There are jobs that we might envy, but we know we'll never have them. It takes faith to believe that God doesn't judge us according to our paychecks, the size of our office, the car we drive, or the spot we park it in. He is the God who chose Gideon and David when they were the youngest and least in their families. God continues to do His work through each of us. What we do with God through our vocation is never a payment for His forgiveness or an advance pay for eternal life. It's our chance to be a child in our Father's family, but a child who is excited to leave the toys and begin to do real work. We aren't perfect, but we're forgiven, and because of His forgiveness, God looks at what we do in our vocation with Him and says, "We did good today."

LET'S HAVE EVERYONE OVER

The first Thanksgiving that a young couple hosts is a major event. It's one thing to bring a store-bought pie to your mother-in-law's house. It's something else to buy the Thanksgiving turkey, remember to start thawing it on Monday morning, and have it all done by 3:00 p.m. Thursday. And don't forget the mashed potatoes, the stuffing, the sweet potatoes, and the cranberries. But when it's done, everyone agrees it was a wonderful meal. Best of all, everyone sat happily an extra hour at the table. That's a family in action.

Our worship services are these family moments acted out each week. We receive the shared meal of the Lord's Supper, the reminder of our Baptism, and the weekly sharing of the Scriptures. We open the door to welcome everyone in the family of God to come. We all share the same story of Jesus' love and His sacrifice that brings each of us into the household of God. Like a good Thanksgiving meal, it includes both the familiar and the new. We're counting on seeing the same people in the same places. But there are also chairs waiting for those coming for the first time, wondering if they can join the family. The answer is yes! We're all family, created and adopted by the same Father and saved by His Son. It is Thanksgiving every Sunday, and there's room for everyone.

1. When you say, "Let's go home," what are the best parts of being home?

2. Worship can be done privately, but how is our Sunday worship richer when we're part of the whole family of God?

3. Worship reminds us through the Absolution, the Bible readings, the sermon, and the Lord's Supper that we're forgiven. Why do we welcome this reassurance coming in so many ways?

4. We noted that worship, both public and private, needs to be done in faith. What aspects of our worship especially call for faith as well as strengthen our faith?

5. What were some of the jobs you did that showed you weren't just a child anymore?

6. God works through our vocations to care for the world. Why would God choose to work through His people and not simply do all His own work by His own direct hand?

7. All our vocations are equally valued by God. When we feel that we're not important, what does God say about us and about what He is doing through us?

RESOURCES

For further study and understanding, please consult the following resources.

Luther's Small Catechism with Explanation (St. Louis: Concordia Publishing House, 2017). See especially the explanation on the Church Year and worship, pages 377–93.

"Living the Wholly Christian Life," in *The Lutheran Study Bible* (St. Louis: Concordia Publishing House, 2009), pages 2138–39.

Lutheran Service Book, hymn 853: "How Clear Is Our Vocation, Lord," and hymn 904: "Blessed Jesus, at Your Word."

CHAPTER 8

LET'S FIND OUR
FOREVER HOME

When Holly and I were first married, we drove a rented truck with all our stuff from Minnesota to our little apartment in Fort Wayne, Indiana. I bet half the weight in that truck came from our sofa sleeper. How could anything covered in cloth feel like concrete? Since we didn't know a soul in Fort Wayne, Holly ended up carrying her half of that couch from the truck into the living room. Someone should have told us that the marriage vows were actually "love, honor, and lift." When we got the couch in, Holly set her half of it down and said, "Before we move this again, you make some friends."

Nevertheless, besides needing some strong-backed friends, that first apartment was all we wanted. A door of our own, with real keys. A living room where we could put the couch and our one chair. A backyard with our own dandelions and crabgrass. We were set.

Of course, soon we wanted more. An apartment is fine for a start, but we moved six times in our first five years of seminary, vicarage, and graduate school. After six moves, we were ready for a house. Every couple wants a place to love and a place to stay. You want walls with no one else on the other side of them. You want a place that's bigger than your moving truck. Let there be an empty bedroom so you can dream of how to fill it. You want a place where you can live and grow.

The relationship God has with us looks for this place to live and grow. Our home with God is where we gather as a family. It's also a place where others can find us. Our congregations and their churches are those homes for us and for everyone seeking that home. Serving us today, they also look forward to the eternal home to which God is bringing us.

It takes faith to see all this when looking at our churches and us. We're not always impressive. Our choir hasn't found perfect pitch. Our acolyte could light only five of the seven candles today. No one is asking for a copy of the sermon or waiting for an encore. But we're still at home here, and we would like others to join us. That's because this is a house built on the relationship God has with us; He is calling us to be His own, and we hear that call by faith. By sight, we're not much, but by faith, we're God's own people in His own place.

> By sight, we're not much, but by faith, we're God's own people in His own place.

Come and join us.

WHEN DOES IT FEEL LIKE HOME?

When you move into a new place, it takes some time before it starts to feel like home. When is that place finally home for you? When you turn automatically into that driveway without thinking? When you paint the living room your own color? When you've unloaded every box and can find four out of five things in a day? Maybe it takes all that and a bit more. But eventually, we go from calling it "the new place" to saying, "We're home."

Our congregations most often find themselves at home in their church building. Certainly, some congregations don't have a traditional church building but flourish in a rented movie theater or a school gym on Sunday morning. But let's focus for a while on the traditional church building that most Lutheran congregations use. It can be white-framed, long and narrow, four stained glass windows on each side, proudly built over a hundred years ago by the great-grandparents of the people who gather there every Sunday. It can be a testimony to the excitement of the baby boom in the 1950s and 1960s, brick walls with blond oak woodwork and hard-back pews. It might be fairly new, a starter building, single story, metal siding for now, but with plans to add a front entry, put up a steeple, and replace the siding with brick. Just like our houses, Lutheran churches come in all colors, shapes, and sizes, and people call each of them home.

What makes them home, and beautiful beyond their shape and size, is what happens inside. Here God creates and strengthens His relationship with us. We have already spoken of worship in the previous chapter, and worship certainly is the center of what draws us together. Much of the church building is structured around Sunday worship. Perhaps there is a cross shape to the sanctuary, a long central aisle with intersecting wings near the front. Or we see the story of the Scriptures through the stained glass windows on either side.

The window depicting Jesus as the Good Shepherd carrying the lamb shines the brightest for you every Sunday. Above the altar hangs a cross, and below it stands a statue of Jesus, welcoming you, the nail marks showing in His hands. The building tells the Gospel story before the opening hymn is sung.

The building tells the Gospel story before the opening hymn is sung.

But there is even more to the beauty and welcome of our building than the 9:00 a.m. worship on Sunday morning. There's the warmth of being greeted at the door and catching up with friends. There's the goodness of seeing the same couple that has come twenty minutes early for church for forty-five years. There's noticing that young man who quietly slides in and goes up to the balcony. He'll leave a bit early, but you're glad to see him here because it's been a while since he's come. It's the wonderful aroma of coffee brewing as you walk in. It's the smell of the potluck dishes being kept warm for the meal after service. Not all this tells the Gospel message completely, but it opens the door and promises that you're welcome here. It takes faith to believe the invitation, but it's true. Trust His call. The door is open.

You're also welcome when we move to a new place or two. As beloved as our church building is, we can hear His Word and be His people in other places as well. The Church is really the people of God found in large and small groups. For example, our church in Butternut, Wisconsin, sent our youth group to the National Youth Gathering held every three years. Some twenty-five to thirty thousand youth attend this wonderful gathering. Our twenty or thirty youth and adults from Butternut were an awestruck part of that whole crowd. The Gathering was a picture of the Church on a scale that they had never seen before. But our youth were also the Church in a different way. To make that trip, the youth group had many fund-raising activities. They held bake sales in which two dozen cookies went for twenty-five dollars! To say thanks, the youth decided to paint the home of an elderly church member who lived two doors down the street. Foolishly, I decided we would do it on the first morning of summer vacation from school. What was I thinking? Who wants to spend the first day of vacation painting a house? But that morning, at 8:00 a.m., eighteen high school students were sitting on the curb in front of the church building, waiting to go. That's the Church—eighteen teenagers painting a house for no pay on their first day of vacation. If you were there that day, you would have wanted to pick up a brush and paint along with them.

So join in. The people of God go beyond the church building walls, and you can be with them. It's like making that apartment your home. It feels like someone else's place until you paint it and clean the carpets. Then, even if the color isn't perfect, it's your color. So help out with the food bank on Saturdays, or give out the box meals at the park on Tuesday evenings. Pick some weeds at the neighborhood garden and meet someone new. Volunteer to be a chaperone on the school day trip next month. Help the residents at the nursing home when the congregation gets its once-a-month time to visit. It takes a bit of courage and faith to make that first step. But perhaps you're already in that group that serves. In that case, be the one who says to a friend, "You might really like this. Want to come with me next week?" Whether you have that personal invitation or you just read about what's happening, take the first step. Walk into that church, pick up a bulletin, and settle in for worship. See those teenagers painting a house, and ask if you can help. You'll find that these are the people of faith that you've been looking for. And they've been looking for you.

NO MORE STARTER HOME—THIS ONE WILL LAST

Your first apartment eventually leads to that first starter house, the one that was a little too small almost from the beginning. Soon, three children came along and needed rooms. Then your mother stayed with you while she recovered from her broken hip. There was that month when your sister had to stay before her house was ready. You're glad to help, but soon that three-bedroom ranch house is feeling like a four-hundred-square-foot tiny house. Besides the lack of room, all those people and the dog have started to wear the house down. Cabinet doors don't close anymore, the refrigerator is making strange noises, and no matter where you put the couch, you can't hide all the stains.

You need a lasting home, a place big enough for everyone and a place that's still looking new. You need a place that always has a spare room so you can truly say, "Stay with us! We have plenty of room." You need a place you'll never outgrow or wear out. You need a marvelous Carpenter to build such a place. You need One who is able not only to lift half a sofa sleeper but also build a lasting home. You need this same One to return to earth then and raise you up to be with Him. This is the certainty that we have through the promises of God. This home on earth that we know now is just our starter house. The everlasting home that He promised is coming.

Our trust in God's lasting home has two dimensions. First, we see a resurrection of our frail bodies to the new creation that God has promised. Paul described this change in terms of going from living in a tent to a lasting house not made with hands (2 Corinthians 5:1–3). Our bodies are like fragile tents, so dependent on the world around us. Give us seventy-two degrees in the shade, and our bodies are happy tents. But move the temperature ten degrees up or down, and we'll be complaining. This tent may last quite a while, but it will always show the years.

Resurrection is more than mending the torn tent. Resurrection has no fear of the future, the tomb, or the dust we'll become. God shows His power through that dust. Paul writes of this contrast, saying, "So it is with the resurrection of the dead. What is shown is perishable; what is raised is imperishable. It is sown in dishonor; it is raised in glory. It is sown in weakness; it is raised in power. It is sown a natural body; it is raised a spiritual body" (1 Corinthians 15:42–44). As we began from the dust of Eden, so we're reborn from the dust of the tomb.

As we began from the dust of Eden, so we're reborn from the dust of the tomb.

What an astonishing change it will be when we are raised to new life with Him. We'll step into His promised world, free from so much that we know here: "He will wipe away every tear from their eyes, and death shall be no more, neither shall there be mourning, nor crying, nor pain anymore, for the former things have passed away" (Revelation 21:4). A life free of these things can only be imagined by His promise and trusted by the gift of faith. But that is exactly our trust. We are raised to a lasting perfection of a new body without the pain we now know so well.

This new life needs then a new home. This is the second dimension of the resurrection promise. Our resurrected body isn't sent back to the earth we've known. When our students come to the university, they often try a new look: different hair, new clothes, and they never mention the nickname they were given in middle school. To match all that's new, they move into our residence halls with new roommates, beds, and schedules. Try something new at the cafeteria—I suggest the Hawaiian pizza—and surprise anyone who knew the old you.

In a similar way, our resurrected bodies have the completely new setting of heaven itself. Those who have passed away in faith are already in heaven. We are assured that when Jesus returns to earth at the end of time, He will bring with Him those who have already died in faith in Him and who are present in heaven now (1 Thessalonians 4:14–16). They are not sleeping but already joining in the praise of God, as we note when we worship with angels, archangels, and all the company of heaven. When Jesus returns, then the final union of God and His people will be done. Revelation 19:6–9 describes this as the marriage supper of the Lamb and His Bride, the Church. This isn't a marriage we only watch, stretching to see a glimpse from the back row. No, this is our union with Christ and the fulfillment of the relationship He purchased from eternity. Well does the angel say, "Blessed are those who are invited to the marriage supper of the Lamb" (Revelation 19:9).

This wonderful promise takes faith. Faith alone can see new bodies from old dust. Faith alone can trust that finally our bodies won't hurt anymore. Relationships won't be torn, and eyes will know no tears.

Relationships won't be torn, and eyes will know no tears.

Faith alone hears these promises of God, centered on His relationship with us through His Son. Because of all that Jesus has already done, His promises are our hope. In this book, we've stressed the Word of God, which promises His grace as the foundation of our relationship. That all comes together with the words of Jesus in Revelation 21: "Also He said, 'Write this down, for these words are trustworthy and true.' And He said to me, 'It is done! I am the Alpha and the Omega, the beginning and the end. . . . The one who conquers will have this heritage, and I will be his God and he will be My son'" (Revelation 21:5–7). This is the relationship God has for us, created by His grace alone, received by faith alone, and trusting His Word alone. This is the essence of our Lutheran understanding of God and His promises. Join us in hearing this Word and trusting these gracious promises, so that you might share in this relationship of God with all His people.

We began this book by asking what things people know about you. Lutherans have these three, Scripture, grace, and faith, which start our portrait. Certainly, there are more things to know about us, but these are a start. I hope that you will continue to grow in the relationship God has with us. Join us in celebrating the announcement of God's mercy, received by faith. That's the beginning of a great portrait, and it's the picture that God has of you.

FIRST MEAL IN OUR NEW HOME

So far, our young couple has grown together in their apartment, but now you've outgrown that little place. It's time to buy that first house! Move in, find the boxes marked "kitchen," and make sure the fridge and stove are working. Now, what should you make for a first meal? You could order in pizza for a night or two, but soon, it's time to start cooking. For that first meal, make the family favorite. Chicken divan casserole, peas and carrots, fresh rolls, and Shenandoah Valley apple cake for dessert (an actual Paavola menu that's worked for almost forty years now). It's a new house, but we're the same family even here.

We gather in our congregations for worship, but we know that a more lasting house and celebration are coming. Now we meet for an hour or two a week; we're moving to a celebration and meal that won't end. Now we're a small circle, but coming is a host of guests that can't be counted. But one thing will be the same. Both here and for eternity, in our temporary home and in the heaven to come, we feast on the words of God and the work of His Son. His words have fed us here, and we'll celebrate them even more when we gather around His throne. If they have filled us with love, joy, and peace here, imagine how rich and satisfying they will be when we settle into our eternal home and circle around His table.

1. When did you move a concrete couch or some other impossible piece of furniture? When did that new place finally feel like home?

2. Church buildings come in many sizes and shapes. They are old and new, small and large. What is your favorite style of church building?

3. When does a church structure go beyond being simply a building to being a living place of God's people?

4. The people of God often meet beyond the church walls. When have you especially benefited from or been part of the life of the church outside the congregation's normal setting?

5. Describe the house or houses in which you grew up. Was this a series of apartments, a first smaller home, or the final stop after many moves?

6. This chapter described some aspects of the wonderful promise of our resurrection. What strikes you as the most amazing and faith-demanding aspect of God's promise to raise us and our very bodies, even from the dust?

7. We want a new, permanent home beyond this earth. Using especially the vision of heaven in Revelation 21–22 and elsewhere, what is most striking and important to you in the description of heaven?

RESOURCES

For further study and understanding, please consult the following resources.

Luther's Small Catechism with Explanation (St. Louis: Concordia Publishing House, 2017). See especially the explanation of the Third Article of the Apostles' Creed and the explanation of the Lord's Prayer, especially the Second and Third Petition.

"What Happens When We Die?" in *The Lutheran Study Bible* (St. Louis: Concordia Publishing House, 2009), page 1750.

Lutheran Service Book, hymn 461: "I Know That My Redeemer Lives," and hymn 672: "Jerusalem the Golden."

NOTES

NOTES

NOTES

NOTES

NOTES